© 2016 Monster Mas Series
All Rights Reserved.

No part of this publication may be reproduced, stored in a retrieval system, or transmitted, in any form or by any means, electronic, mechanical, photocopying, recording, or otherwise, without the written permission of the author.

ISBN: 978-1-7363919-2-1

This book is printed on acid-free paper.

This book is a work of fiction. Places, events, and situations in this book are purely fictional and any resemblance to actual persons, living or dead, is coincidental.

Printed in the United States of America

In memory of my loving father,
Philip John Arabadjis.
The quest for knowledge
is the best gift you've ever given to me!

Heather Arabadjis writes fun and exciting children's books about real issues elementary and middle school students face in education today. Her *Monster Mas* series is widely loved by young readers, helping them understand and handle in positive ways bullying, testing anxiety, and even school politics. In her fourteen years teaching public school in New York City, Heather has passionately empowered youth to achieve a college education or better, advocating as a teacher and writer that hard work, self-control, cooperativeness, and being nice do pay off. In visits to schools and communities throughout her career, she has inspired countless students by sharing her personal story of rising from urban poverty to academic and creative success.

"Good morning class!" Mr. Washington greeted his fourth grade students. "What an important time of the year - we're going to choose or 'elect' a school president!"

"Huh . . . what does a school president do?" Mas was interested.

"They are leaders with huge responsibility," Mr. Washington replied. "They speak for all the students."

"I was born a leader," Ronald said proudly. "When I was just two years old, I led a group of over 300 to build a wall for protection."

"Wow, Ronald, that's impressive," Mr. Washington remarked as some students nodded approvingly.

"Two years old . . . *hmmphh*," Jill said skeptically. "You had 300 other toddlers at your command - there is a legal age to work in this country, you know," Jill picked at him.

"Ronald didn't work with babies, they were ants," Vern chided.

"Zip it! Quiet! Silence!" Ronald demanded. "If I say it's so, you can take it to the bank."

"Whatever Ronald says, just what I thought," Jill said, unimpressed.

"You're a non-believer!" Ronald didn't like criticism. "I got them to build this wall by their ant hill; they were having too many floods, and had to keep rebuilding their home."

Mr. Washington tried to get things back on track, "Well, Ronald you describe an essential quality of a good leader - finding solutions."

Ronald grinned, flattered. The teacher continued, "Another great quality of a leader is working side-by-side with a team. Take the principal of this school; he doesn't run it by himself. Who else do you think helps him?"

"The assistant principal," Vern called out.

"The teachers, counselors, and lunch aides," Mas offered. "They've all helped me, so that's helping the principal, since kids are why he's here."

"Good thinking Mas," Mr. Washington commended.

"Yeah, whatever," Ronald didn't like that Mas had the teacher's attention.

"Also, to be a good leader, you must be really familiar with your school," Mr. Washington went on. "Anyone running for president must be enrolled in the school for three years, and be at least ten years old."

Some students looked upset. One kid called out, "That's not fair, I just moved here."

"I'm sorry, and though I understand your disappointment, I don't make the rules," Mr. Washington explained. "Ok, class, let's take a look at this slide show I've prepared about our past presidents. Please use the graphic organizer to fill in the columns on the positive, and, as you will see, negative effects these presidents had on the school. Then, when we finish, we'll line up for gym."

When they finished the exercise, the class lined up noisily. "Move!" Ronald ordered as he pushed his way into the line.

"You know, if I were president, I would put a stop to bullying," Mas said quietly to Jeremiah.

"What's that, you president???" Ronald overheard, "What a joke!" he barked at Mas.

"Yeah, and what's your plan as president, Mr. Big Shot?" Mas snapped back.

The rest of the class had tuned into their conversation.

"Ronald, really, what would be your platform?" Jill asked.

"I don't wear platform shoes; that's what you girls wear to pretend you're taller," Ronald smirked.

"Seriously?" Jill tried not to respond nastily. "Look, your platform is what you believe will help the school, the actions you will take to get to those goals, part of your overall campaign," Jill explained thoughtfully.

"Wait, wait! Camping? I'm in!" Vern said excitedly.

"Vern, not camping, 'campaigning'," she corrected, rolling her eyes a bit, "it's the process of getting elected." She looked at the boys and said to herself, *What amateurs.*

"Hey, hey, I have some experience with that," Vern was so eager. "I was mayor for the Burlington Boys club three times in a row. And you know what? If I were president, I would save this school a lot of money, and even help save the earth."

"Super Vern!" a kid joked.

"How so?" Jill asked.

"You know how your parents are always telling you to shut off the lights after yourself, and to turn off the faucet when you're brushing your teeth, and other stuff like that? Well, our school needs to do more conservation, we can 'Go Green'!"

"Super Fern!" Ronald sniggered, "give us a break."

"Ronald," Vern was flustered, "you sure like to pick on people. But you haven't said one thing you would do for our school."

"*Um, um . . .*" Ronald tried to come up with something fast. He glanced at Eduardo, a new student. "I know! The teacher said that kids couldn't run for president if they weren't here for at least three years. They shouldn't get other privileges, either. Like, they shouldn't get the same one-to-one time with the teacher, so all of us who started here from the beginning can learn more. If they don't like it, we should make them go back to school where they came from."

"You'll do what?" Eduardo said angrily, and he and a few other new students glared at Ronald, who just ignored them.

'Phloooweeeee! Phloooweeeee!' a whistle blew loudly as the class entered the gym. "Settle down students and take your assigned spots, please," Mr. Roosevelt, the gym teacher directed. "Today we are going to form teams."

"*Yesss*! I already got my top picks. They're good in every sport," Ronald bragged.

"It's campaign teams, though, that we're picking today," Mr. Roosevelt clarified. "I heard you guys going at it about politics as you came in, so you know it's school election time. When you're on a team you have to work together to achieve a desired goal. So, who's running in the primaries?"

Students looked at each other, confused.

"I don't know anything about the primaries, but I'm running for President," Ronald declared.

"Me too!" Vern announced.

"Count me in!" added Mas.

"You boys are so clueless," Jill chided, but not saying if she was interested. She thought to herself, *I can't believe we have had only boys running our school*. Still, she liked to be helpful, so she explained - "This is how it works: each grade, third through fifth, chooses one candidate to run for President. These are our primaries. Then when it's election time, all eligible students can choose from the candidates who win the primaries. It's rare that the third graders have a candidate to run because they are overwhelmed with the third grade exam, and are still getting their feet wet anyway."

Yeah, I should know, Mas thought to himself, *that test anxiety is no joke. Thank goodness I learned how to get rid of the Thark, that nasty test monster.*

"Very good, Jill, you took the words right out of my gym bag," Mr. Roosevelt complimented her. He got ready to throw dodge balls with pictures on them. "Now, when I count to three, I want you all to pick one ball with the picture that describes your personality." The kids were ready to race to the balls. "Okay, one . . . two . . . THREEEEEEEEEE!!!"

"I'm getting the first one!" Ronald picked it up and saw a colorful butterfly on it. "Not! That's definitely a girl thing," and he tossed the ball away and ran to another.

"This one's mine," Mas said holding onto a ball with art utensils on it, as other students scrambled about laughing and jostling each other in this funny game.

"Time's up!" Mr. Roosevelt shouted and everyone sort of froze. "All the art or what I like to call 'Creative' ball holders come stand here, 'Social Butterflies' over here, 'Mathicals', the balls with numerical symbols here, and 'Directors', you can tell, here."

"Hey, cool, Jer, you're on my team." Mas and his friend did a secret hand shake and ended it with a high five.

"Chris, switch balls with someone, come to my Directors group," Ronald demanded.

"Guys, there will be no switching!" Mr. Roosevelt ordered. "You will notice you have friends in some of your groups, and that's normal because friends usually have things in common. But in order to have an effective campaign team, you need one person from each group. Let's do a quick rundown of each, and then I'll let you go."

Are you a Director, let's see,
Can you come up with a plan?
Make sure you involve your team,
Train, guide, delegate as the point man.

Jill interrupted, "Huh? *Hmmm* . . . point person."

Mr. Roosevelt acknowledged Jill with a nod, and continued.

Creatives come up with ideas
To get the campaign message across,
By using newspapers, television, and art,
They make their candidate boss!

Social butterflies, everyone loves them,
They talk up ideas and get students real amped;
By organizing events to promote them,
They ensure their candidate is the champ!

Mathicals, oh how we need them!
It's not easy to work up and keep a budget,
To fund programs and activities at school,
Don't ask me why, but most students have fudged it.

"So, I can't be on Mas' team?" Jer asked.

"Of course you can, this is a class exercise. You can help his campaign team if you want," Mr. Roosevelt reassured.

"Oh, cool, that was a close one Jer," Mas was relieved.

"Yeah, and Chris can be on my team, too," said Ronald.

All the students were buzzing about their teams as they left gym. The class was high energy and full of chatter as they entered Mr. Washington's room. "I bet you enjoyed Mr. Roosevelt's gym class on team-building for the elections," he said as they settled down. "Before you leave for the day, I've given you some reading about our school elections as part of homework. If you decide to run, there is a sheet you can submit tomorrow to enter the process officially, and of course you have to get one of your parent's signature."

Ronald looked down dejectedly, and Mas couldn't help but notice.

At home, Mas ran up to his mother, "Mom, I got to tell you something! I'm thinking about running for school president!"

"Wow, that's wonderful, honey bunny. I always knew you were a little leader. When you first learned your A B C's, you made sure all the other babies would say clearly, L,M,N,O,P. It was so funny how you tots used to say that; it sounded like *lemonpee. Ha ha!*"

"Mom, c'mon, be serious. I don't know anything about being a good president. This is all new to me."

"Don't be intimidated by a challenge, Massimo. You can learn from past presidents, from reading, and online videos, I know you love watching them."

"I tried to do that, but on my tablet when I typed 'super delegate' from Mr. Washington's exercise, it showed only super heroes . . . and of course I had to watch them for a while," he said grinning.

"*Ohhh*, you rascal. Let me try to help. Let me read the teacher's exercise to check how your school does it." Mas' mother took in the information really quickly. "*Hmm*, it's a bit more complicated at your school. Since each grade is voting to select one candidate who will run against the other grades, the super delegates from each grade generally support the candidate they think has the best chance of winning overall."

"Doesn't each kid get a vote too, and aren't there more total kids than super delegates?"

"Yes to both questions, honey. Usually, in our national elections, super delegates support the majority vote, that is the candidate with the most popular votes, but that doesn't happen all the time."

"Who are my school's super delegates?"

"In your school, according to this, they would be students who have been allowed to work with administration. Does your school have a safety officer patrolling the halls?"

"No, I wish they did, then I wouldn't have been bullied."

"Mas, are you still being bullied?" his mother asked with worry.

"No, not really, it's nothing. I think I know a super delegate, a girl who works in the principal's office."

"Yes, exactly. But honey bunny, Mas, about bullying or any other problems, you know you can tell me anything."

"I do Mom, I know you got my back."

Vern also was excited about running for president.

"Mom! Dad! You've always said I can make this world a better place, right?"

"Yes!" they responded as one.

"Then tomorrow I'm going to start my campaign for school president. What do you think of that? I need your help. We give in our official slips tomorrow; I want to start campaigning right away!"

His father reviewed the election paperwork. "It says here that you have to submit your forms first, but it doesn't say you have to wait to get started campaigning."

"Yes!!! And guess what my platform is?"

"Tell us Vern!"

"Conserving, reusing, and recycling! Thank you so much for teaching me how important that is."

"That's right son, if we don't take care of our planet now," his mother said with concern, "we won't have a world to live in."

"My school wastes so much of its resources," Vern said, irritated. "I think I can save us lots of money, and use it on other things the school needs." He was psyched as his Mom and Dad each signed the permission slip.

Jill could barely contain her enthusiasm when she walked in her house.

"Mom, Dad, I've been waiting for this for years! I'm running for school president! I couldn't really run last year because the mandatory third grade test was pretty tough. But this year I'm on top of things."

"That's great Hun, have you told your cousin Phil? He was president at your school some years back."

"Yes, Mom, he's coming over, and he's bringing some kids that helped him win."

"Jill," her mother looked at her warily, "one important thing about running for president is to run an honest campaign. No matter what, never lie. Even if your opponents are liars, they will get caught."

"Yes, mom, I know, 'honesty is the best policy'." She looked at her mother, remembering the way she herself had lied about seeing some students sneak out of school, a few of whom almost drowned at the local pond where they went. Jill didn't say anything back then because she didn't want to be called a 'snitch'.

"Jill, even though you weren't to blame for those kids leaving the school," her mother zeroed in, "you could've helped prevent the trouble that happened. And how their parents must have felt, I can't imagine," she said and squeezed Jill close to her.

Jill looked down, "Maybe I can make it up; I'll campaign with, 'Honesty saves lives'."

"That's a bit dramatic; why not, 'An Honest Try Beats a Lie', something like that?"

"That's a great idea," Jill said pleased.

●●●●● $-Mobile　　　　9:30 PM　　　　🠕 ✳ 95% 🔋

< Messages　　　　**Dad**　　　　Details

> Hey Dad r u up? 🤑😊

Yes son, dinner with clients, but got a minute or two 🍾 🍴

> Where are you dad?

🇨🇭, tomorrow I fly to 🇫🇷

> I want to run for school president 👑

Great son 👍, I know you will do great, will hire someone to work with you on your campaign, don't worry about 💰

> Ok Dad, I wish you were here 🙇

Me too son but let me know when the elections are so I can calendar it in 📅

> Ok, ttyl 😁

Gn 😪

iMessages

The next day, loads of second and third graders crowded around Vern in the cafeteria, signing up to join his Green Team.

"Vote for EnVERNoment, Vote for EnVERNoment!" kids chanted as they thrust up handmade signs.

"Hey," Mas was dumbfounded as he walked in from the playground, "what are you doing, the elections didn't start yet? You're not playing fair Vern."

"There were no rules about when we could begin our campaigns, I just got an early start."

Mas slumped away, not wanting to start another scene about politics. But he didn't like that he was already behind in the race. He felt bad pressure inside, so he let a fart out slow and sneaky, that usually helped. It was nothing like his awful Fartnado, but still . . .

"Pee-yuu, who let that monster out?!!"

Vern gagged holding his nose as other kids bolted from the table to escape the rotten smell.

Hmm, silent but deadly, Mas had a monstery smirk. *Works every time.*

The bell rang and children flooded into the school from playing outside. They congregated in the halls reading the school newspaper, with all eyes looking up as Mas walked along.

"What's going on Jer? Do I have food on my face again," Mas asked, then thought to himself, *There's no way they figured out that fart was from me; silent, like I said.*

Mas looked in shock at the front of the newspaper Jer handed him. There he was, on the front page, grunting on the potty! He started running away down the hallway as children pointed and mocked and hooted.

What in a democratic socialist revolution?!!! How did someone get this picture? It was only on my laptop . . . the Cloud, uh oh! Jer warned me about the Cloud. The hallway seemed to start spinning, and Mas noticed his reflection in a window – he was getting monstery by the minute! *NO, NOT AGAIN!!!* Mas ran out of the school as students howled in laughter. He ran through the schoolyard and playing fields straight into the woodlands next to the school. Mas ran as hard as he could, feeling so much shame and dread.

"I can never go back to school; my life is O-VERRRR!"

he exclaimed in misery. He suddenly tripped on a rock and banged his head hard on the ground. "*Unnhh, uhhhh*, stupid rock," he said angrily. He picked it up with both hands and hurled it away. It landed with a big splash in a small pond.

"*DUDE!!!* What's your problem?" someone croaked annoyedly.

"*Whahhh*? Where did this pond come from?" Mas stepped beside the deep green water. He looked down at the surface, and there was Monster Mas staring up at him! "NO!!! I was just trying to do something good for the school!" he screamed.

"*Yo, Yo, Yo, calma te chico, calma te*. Like I said, why are you blowing up my spot? And who are you talking to? Really kid, a one-on-one with yourself? Aren't you on social media for this kind of thing?"

"Who's there?!!!" Monster Mas yelled with surprise.

"Yo! Down here, He Who Tosses Big Rocks Before Thinking." It was a big slimy green bullfrog.

"A frog? Oh boy, am I totally losing it?" Monster Mas was freaking out.

"If anyone's losing it, it's me," croaked the frog, "talking to a pre-pubescent monster."

"I'm not a monster, I'm a boy!"

"Let's pretend I'm the prince, and a princess is looking to kiss me. Seen any of that lately? Not! But you? Definitely *Scary Movie* style. Listen, we all have our problems, but it's not something we run from."

"How do you know I'm running away? Monsters live in the forests; not so weird."

"Yeah, yeah, and under the bed too. What's your deal, kid?"

"Well, I'm running for school president, or at least I was planning too. But this boy Vern got a head start in the campaign, everyone cheering *EnVernoment*, and someone found a picture of me on the potty, and now I'm a laughingstock, a joke."

"That's it? Wish I had your problems. Up to today, I have almost been eaten 24 times, eighteen of them was when I was just a tadpole. Some will try to wipe you out, and certainly put you down, especially when you're in competition. Vern's slogan? Good marketing, totally fair play. Potty paparazzi? That's 'dirty politics'. Be positive about it, though, have a sense of humor, show the voters you can handle anything."

"*Hmmm* . . . I suppose you're right."

"Told you I was a prince, I know a few things about politics. How I ended up this way is another, old story. Now go the way you came. You should come to your senses pretty soon. Anything I said that helps you, remember it."

"Thanks Froggy," and Mas let out a little gas in appreciation, "how's that for coming to my senses?"

"Not what I meant; a funky dude, you are, Monster Mas. Try this slogan against your opponents, 'There's More With Mas', short and sweet."

"Ight, I'll think about it, Prince of Frogs."

21

Monster Mas sat up groggily from the forest floor. He had a good-sized bump on his head. "*What the..?* He sadly realized he had become monstery like in the past when he got super-stressed. He thought of his bizarre encounter with the frog, but was more worried about missing school and falling even farther behind in the campaign. He rushed back to campus and found the hallways empty; classes were all in session. *What should I do? I can't just walk into my classroom; I would have to get a late pass. I need a distraction... I know what! I've been practicing at home.* Monster Mas grabbed his lunchbox in the cubby outside Mr. Washington's room. He swallowed a mouthful of sparkling water.

There's a lot at stake, my weird little friend,
let the side effects be minimal;
welcome to town, my new Burp Quake,
Hope I don't get caught by the principal!

As Monster Mas let out the awful burp, the building started to shake!

"Everyone under your desks; it's an earthquake!!!" Principal Lincoln shouted into the P.A. microphone as he dove beneath his work table.

"*Whoah!*" cried Monster Mas, wobbling to his classroom a few doors away as the hallway still swayed, "my *Burp Quake* even has an aftershock!" He peeked in his class and saw everyone huddled scared under their desks. The teacher wasn't looking his way. "Here's my chance," and Monster Mas folded himself up really tightly and rolled like a pinball underneath his desk.

When the Burp Quake finally subsided, Principal Lincoln's worried voice came on the P.A. – "Students, that wasn't an earthquake, we were the only ones in the area to feel it. We'll find out what it was. But for now, let's get back to work, and whatever you are, be a good one!"

"Alright class, you heard the boss. Given the time, I'm gonna cut to the quick of my curriculum." Mr. Jackson began,

There's something called a budget,
it's very important to know;
so much depends on these digits,
books, food, teachers, even shows.

These numbers say what we should be doing,
and don't believe them? something might get cut;
last year, it was our class for cooking,
this year we hope to avoid this somewhat!

"Our past school's presidents haven't understood about balancing the budget, and the school has to keep cutting programs," Vern spoke up. "If I become president, I plan to know all the current programs, see just how much money they need, and have us be part of any decisions about them!"

"Yeah!" students liked a lot the idea of being involved in decisions.

"Hey, Mr. Jackson, is there any way we students can raise money to keep programs running?" Mas asked.

"Yes, Mas, that's called fundraising, and it's very important to leadership. You can host events such as car washes, candy sales, and many others to benefit the school. For these elections, there is always a special reserve fund to promote your campaign using posters, and you can run free ads in the newspaper and even on the school news channel. Let's play a game that will help with your campaign."

"Awesome. I'll take budgets for $200."

"Well, I don't need to raise money," Ronald boasted, "I'll just use the money I have in one of my accounts. And my dad already donates to the school."

"Oh, so that's why you always get your lunch and snacks before the rest of us," Monster Mas said bitingly.

"Money talks!" Ronald flaunted.

Well, money can't buy you skills, Monster Mas said to himself, *game on!*

A way-out vision of the election contest flashed in Monster Mas' imagination:

He transformed into a space fighter, with a white gown and blue light saber, ready to battle Ronald, who had transformed too.

Ronald opened his diabolical red light saber, *Pshshshshshsh*! "Go back to your potty on Pluto!" he violently struck Monster Mas' saber, forcing him backwards.

"You're a politician from the dirty side, I know it was you that smeared me in the paper, but one bad pic can't hurt me!"
Monster Mas leaped forward and his blue saber sparked against Ronald's burning red blade.
"You have a lousy platform with no good activities. I'm proposing fun Fridays in the empire, and we're all going to bring a baby picture in to warrior training."
Monster Mas stuck out his tongue as he struck again and again with his saber. He spotted some of the super delegates watching the fight from their hovercrafts.
"I must win this battle!" he declared fiercely.

But just then, Vern jumped into the fight with his glowing green light saber.
"Fix the school, I will. Much to learn, you still have. Fix, wasting resources, we do; I will, yes. Whooosaaahhh…"

The fourth grade boys were locked in a ferocious three-way battle for president of the empire!

"Ha ha ha! I'm Princess Jill, I can fight too!"
and she lit up her hot pink saber.
"Girls in the empire aren't treated equally; I will get rid of boy programs with low attendance. I will get more girl super delegates in the main office!"

The light sabers clashed together and appeared for a moment as a wildly twisting rainbow.

"Enough of this game, now feel the dirty power!"
Ronald sneered as he dropped his saber then lifted his hands and thrust them at his opponents. They all fell back from his foul energy blast.

Ronald transformed into a colossal intergalactic tablet that looked like an enormous black mirror floating in space. "I am Ronatron," he declared, shooting out thermonuclear sparks, "and I will bring this school into the technological age. Every classroom will be a massive laptop, and we'll have us some cute-looking cyborg teachers."

"There's not enough money in the budget to do that," Masssimas Primo returned fire from a smart phone the size of a king-sized bed, "but if I can swing a crush fundraiser, maybe we can at least have access to tablets during center time."

"What?!! No girl transformers in this future?" space renegade Jill Fox shouted, "I'm hot as Venus and I wear the coolest clothes. Ronatron, or whatever your dumb name is, go ahead and try to buy students' votes, because then you will have to keep buying things for the school with your own money, and I've heard the few Martian lemonade stands you own are sinking fast."

"Ahhhhhhhrrrrrrgggggghhhh!!!"

Ronatron roared as he shot some red hot atoms Jill Fox's way.

Jill Fox fast & furiously fled the scene. Meanwhile Data Vector Vern scampered by wildly on a spaceboard and crashed right into Ronatron's hyper-USB port –

KABLAAAAMMMM!!!

"Earth to Mas!" Ronald was grilling Monster Mas as he snapped out of his daydreaming. He heard his name being called on the P.A. along with Ronald's, Jill's, and Vern's. *Please report to the Student Body President's room,* the office directed them.

When they all gathered there, they saw current school president Barry who motioned for them to join him. "This a very crucial time," he began enthusiastically, "students will be voting soon, and they and the super delegates will determine who gets to be the presidential candidate from the fourth grade."

Jill spoke up, "Can you help us with some advice?"

"Sure, I'll take a question from each of you."

Vern rudely jumped in first ahead of Jill, who just frowned. "You see, all the students like what I have to say, and pledge to vote for me, but how do I get these super delegates to like me?"

"Well, that's a tough one, Vern. I had a similar issue, and it looked like I was going to lose, but I kept working harder and harder, and when those super delegates saw that the majority of students were on my side, they supported me as their candidate."

"I have been working hard, Mr. President!"

"It looks like it Vern, from what I've seen of your campaign."

"*Hmmphh,* I don't have to worry too much about those delegates," Ronald said smugly.

"Did you buy them out already?" Monster Mas took a dig at him.

"No, my dad messaged me that the team that likes elephants should always win."

"*Huh?* What team am I on then?" Vern asked, even more confused.

"The dummy team, *ha ha ha!*" Ronald chortled.

"Typically in our school politics," Barry explained, "there's been voters who believe students should have more choices, while others believe in being a bit more strict about things. You kind of appeal to one voting 'bloc', or 'constituency' or the other. Now, *hmm,* Ronald, your question?"

"Well, I don't really need to ask a question, but I noticed that some students don't like what I have to say, and I'd still like to win them over."

"I don't think you can win everyone's vote," Barry replied, "because students have many different opinions. You need to find out what's most important to your school and talk about those things. If you haven't already done so, poll the students about what matters to them, use the results, and promote things that are important to the school."

"Well, I proposed that students who didn't start in our school don't get the same services and attention, and some kids liked it, but, a lot of kids didn't."

"I'm not surprised by that," Barry replied.

"I guess I should change some things before elections next week."

"It's never too late to improve your message Ronald."

"Jill, your question?"

"Well, I want a little advice as well," Jill said, pretending she wasn't bothered about not going first. "I may have said something in the past that wasn't entirely true, but at the time I didn't know what else to say. Some students who know about it keep spreading around what I did. I want to change my reputation, so my classmates can trust and vote for me."

"Well, being honest is very important, no one likes a liar. If you've ever lied to your parents before, and they knew you were lying, what did you do?" Barry asked without being mean.

"Tell the truth," Monster Mas answered.

"Exactly, apologize and explain why you lied, tell the truth and promise you will never do it again."

"Yeah, and didn't your cousin Phil the president get the peach when he lied?" Ronald asked snidely.

"Well, Ronald it's actually called 'being impeached'," Barry explained, "and when you lie when you are President, you can be removed this way. Phil had to go through a long process, but at the end he finished his term."

"I will not make the same mistake, guaranteed," Jill remarked, and gave Ronald a disapproving look.

"Mas, anything from you?"

Monster Mas shook his head, "Nah, I'm good." The other candidates were shocked Mas didn't have a question. Ronald looked especially nervous about it.

"Okay, let's wrap this up guys," Barry spoke like an adult. "Don't forget to use a catchy slogan that all students can relate to; mine was 'Barry Brings Better'. And that's exactly what I did, since I left the school with the Llama Care Medical facility."

"Oh, that's excellent, that's why we have cool band aids that actually stay on your skin," Monster Mas said.

"No, it's not cool, it costs the school a lot of money to run," Ronald protested, "and a lot of students don't even use the medical office. I've been in this school for six years, and haven't needed to go there once."

"Well, Ronald everyone is entitled to his opinion, but accidents do happen, and if they do, the school is 100% equipped to help you. Anyways, times up. Good luck!" Barry said and the group filed out to return to their classroom.

"What a real dude," Monster Mas said to his fellow candidates. "Gotta get busy!"

After a few weeks of polling, explaining, promoting, and campaigning, it was time for the rivals to compete for votes in the big debate in the school auditorium.

"Hello fourth grade students!" Principal Lincoln warmly called from the stage to the student assembly. "Today the final four fourth grade candidates will give a speech. After each speech you can load questions into our new election app and have them answered by the candidates. Then on election day, you decide who will run for school president from your class year. Our first candidate up is Vern."

"Testing one, testing two," Vern spoke loudly, tapping the mic. Then he began.

"Hello, everyone! Did you know we have a growing population of students who can't read? Pre-K should know their letters, and sounds; Kinders should be able to read two to three sentences in a small book, and first graders should be on reading level I. To say the least, Pre- Kinders leave their grade not even knowing how to tie their shoes.

"Class sizes in our school are too big, and students are falling behind academically. We need to have more teachers to reduce class size. We can raise money for this by cutting 10% from each extra curricular activity. To show you an example: to get 10% from the art budget, if all students used the crayons to the very end for the entire year, I bet we could hire one extra teacher. I found so, so, so many wasted crayons in the garbage bin, which brings me to my next point."

"Garbage," Ronald ridiculed under his breath.

"*Shhhh!*" the principal gave him a sharp look.

"We should have an environmental movement. We can help the school conserve, recycle, and reuse its resources. We can start by making a food garden using the empty space on the side of the school. This project won't cost the school any money because my parents are helping me apply for a grant to give the school money to start. We can grow fruits and vegetables for our school lunches. We all need to start eating healthy, there's too much junk food out there.

"A really smart, good, green future is in your hands! Vote EnVernonment!"

Vern finished, and loud applause followed him to his seat with the others on stage.

"Great job Vern!" Principal Lincoln exclaimed. "Next up we have Ronald," and he seemed a little anxious as he grinned taking the microphone from him.

"Hey, students, teachers, who ever else is here. First problem I'm going to solve? We are getting too many students from other schools. That's why we have oversized classes and the younger grades failing."

Most of the audience was already sure of what he was going to say, and they just made 'whatever' faces.

"I alone can solve this problem. Just check the state funds for each student. Did you know the state government gives each school thousands of dollars for each student, and is supposed to give more when enrollments go up? I asked my Dad, and he asked his people in the government. If we have more students, then we should get more money. We can use this money to hire new teachers, without taking away from any programs."

The students' faces suddenly showed surprise, then great interest.

"Next, as president, I would cut Llama Care and use that money for something else. Not everyone needs to go to the nurse - I have been in this school for six years and haven't been to the nurse once. Maybe we can share a nurse with other schools in our district, or get parent volunteers who are nurses or whatever.

"As I was saying, we can use that money to go on more class trips. I don't know why those were cut, I learned the most when I was on them."

"Remodel with Ronald!" he shouted and many, many other students called his name amidst loud and long applause as he sat to rejoin the other candidates.

Wow, I can't believe Ronald changed his approach; he actually has a much better chance of winning now, Monster Mas thought to himself.

"Nice Job Ronald, we never know what to expect from you, do we?" Mr. Lincoln said a bit confused. "Now, here is our next candidate, Jill."

"Good afternoon everyone, I would like to share with you my proposals to help make this school the best place for everyone. How? By making sure everyone is treated equally!"

"Did you know that girls here receive 21% less funding for their school programs than boys? The boys' budget, and I call it this because the following school programs take up the majority of our extracurricular money - football, baseball, basketball, and soccer. The first three sports don't even allow girls to try out, and currently there is only one girl player on the soccer team, and they have her benched the whole game."

"Meanwhile, the following programs have been cut: cooking, fashion design, dance, and tennis. All of these were attended mostly by girls in our school. If we take out one of the boys' sports, we can fund all four of these programs, and all students can enjoy them if they like."

"Boys can't stand that stuff," Ronald interrupted.

A boy from the audience cried out, "What's wrong with cooking? My mom calls me a great chef!"

"Excuse me boys, Jill isn't finished, please be respectful," Principal Lincoln tried to keep order.

"If we choose not to cut anything," Jill continued passionately, "then let the entire student body be part of a fundraiser to bring back programs girls especially want. But the boys have to help too! Most importantly, we have to be fair."

"Another thing I would like to change are the punishment rules in the school. The punishments for school infractions are different in every classroom. For the same infraction of not completing homework, one student could get a week's lunch duty from one teacher, and another teacher can give two weeks' lunch duty. I polled students, and many felt they were treated unfairly based on lateness, missing homework, talking in the classroom, and for accusations of fighting with another student. We should have a system of fair and equal punishments under a judicial system led by OUR PEERS along with teachers. This is OUR school and we should help decide each others' fates justly!"

"VOTE FOR JUSTICE, VOTE FOR JILL!" she ended with gusto, her fist in the air, and rejoined the other candidates.

Students clapped and hooted, her supporters held up her signs chanting wildly, 'JILL! JILL! JILL! while others jeered and acted rudely and said mean things out loud, especially Ronald's followers.

"Whew!!! What a great Job Jill! Principal Lincoln gushed. "Now, last, but certainly not least, we have Mas."

It's the real deal now, no more silly daydreams, Mas, you can do this, he told himself to ward off the anxiety. He stood there nearly strangling the microphone for a few moments in front of his peers.

"*Umm,* hi everyone, and welcome," Monster Mas began nervously. He paused and looked around.

"Are you going to do it or not?" Ronald prodded rudely.

"*Um, yeah, uh...*" and Monster Mas took a big breath. "Bullying is a huge and growing problem in this school. When I came here, I became a victim of bullying. I was very mad and upset. I kept thinking of why this was happening. Not only to me, but to other students as well. I figured out the answer to end bullying, and that is to help the bully."

"What, no way! We should get rid of the bullies!" Eduardo yelled from the audience while looking right at Ronald who was sneering from the stage.

"Getting rid of the bullies from the school won't stop bullying," Mas continued. "What we all need to understand is that the bully is the one that has the problem. If we can figure out what his or even sometimes her problem is, then we can help them. I want to organize a student-led group called 'Bully Aide Crew'. By helping the bullies know that we care about them, we can end bullying and have each other's 'BAC'!"

Ronald's face was turning red, he wanted to say something so badly, but struggled to show everyone he could control his temper.

That's a cool acronym, Jill thought as other students clapped loudly in approval. "Ok, last thing I want to change is the level of fun in this school. I mean we should be able to decide and vote on what activities we have, just like we vote for our president. The polls I conducted tell me many of you want more fun programs and activities. I am going to organize an activities team or for short, the 'A Team'. Their responsibility is to gather your ideas, have students vote on them, and see if the budget can make it happen. How do a video game club, dance club, and cooking club sound? Don't worry about cutting anything out, I have an account on *crowdgivesyoumoney.com*. Plenty of adults will pay for this if they see we are serious and organized. I should know, they helped me start my new rock band, 'Monster Maniacs'.

"Mas Means More!" and Monster Mas dropped the mic on stage then pumped his fist as he left the podium.

"I gave him that one," croaked the Frog Prince who had hopped in for the speeches, startling the boy sitting next to him on the auditorium floor.

"Let's give all of our candidates a much deserved round of applause!" Principal Lincoln shouted excitedly. "What a wonderful job kids! Each one of you has offered such interesting ideas and shown such good leadership."

Monster Mas felt proud of himself - Even if I don't win, I know I gave it my best, just like my Dad would always tell me. He would be proud! And with this thought POOF! He was no longer a monster.

"We'll be hearing from other grades' candidates over the next few days, then voting will take place Tuesday in two weeks in the gym. Good luck candidates!"

All the candidates stood there proudly, ready to work even harder for victory!

AUTHOR'S NOTE

Monster Mas Runs for President introduces fourth through sixth grade students to the thinking and realities of political leadership in school and society. The book ties into my engaging teaching materials about, among other topics, the primary process, campaigning, leadership, platforms, elections, delegates, budgeting, and ethics and fair play. As a home instruction teacher for K through 12 students, including those with special needs, I'd long sought effective ways to enrich instruction for the Social Studies and United States History curricula required for the New York State Regents Exam. How best to create sustained interest in the policies and decisions of presidents and other national leaders, as well as the most important events, challenges, and laws dating from our country's founding to the present? My goal with this book and my other stimulating materials is to get young people more involved with politics as an academic subject and as a crucial part of their future that they can improve upon. My dynamic Regents-focused curriculum is available free by subscribing to my email list at www.Monstermas.com.